ALL YEAR ROUND

Autumn

by

Emilie Dufresne

BookLife
PUBLISHING

©2018
BookLife Publishing
King's Lynn
Norfolk PE30 4LS

All rights reserved.
Printed in Malaysia.

A catalogue record for this book is available from the British Library.

ISBN: 978-1-78637-402-8

Written by:
Emilie Dufresne

Edited by:
Kirsty Holmes

Designed & Illustrated by:
Danielle Jones

IMAGE CREDITS

Cover – Khannanova Margarita. 4 – Inara Prusakova. 5 – Gelpi. 6 – Evgeny Atamanenko. 7 – K Woodgyer. 8 – Purino. 10 – Rawpixel.com. 11 – Tanachot Srijam. 12 – wael alreweie. 14 – ER_09. 15 – Amawasri Pakdara. 16 – Mladen Zivkovic. 18 – Chris Keenan Photography. 19 – Ligak, Ivaylo Ivanov. 20 – Matauw. 22–23 – mandritoiu. Illustrations by Danielle Jones. Images are courtesy of Shutterstock.com. With thanks to Getty Images, Thinkstock Photo and iStockphoto.

CONTENTS

Words that look like this can be found in the glossary on page 24.

It's Autumn!

Crunch! Crunch! The leaves are changing colour and falling to the ground. It must be… autumn!

Autumn is a season of the year. Seasons change when the weather changes. Every season is different.

Summer

Autumn

Spring

Winter

Autumn Weather

HAVE YOU EVER PLAYED IN THE RAIN?

In autumn, the <u>temperature</u> starts to get colder. There can be a lot of rain and wind.

6

In autumn, the days start to feel shorter. This is because there are fewer hours of light in a day.

Autumn
Clothes

HOW MANY TYPES OF <u>WATERPROOF</u> CLOTHES CAN YOU SEE IN THIS PICTURE?

In autumn, we need to wear warmer clothes and waterproofs so we do not get wet or cold!

That's right. There are three!

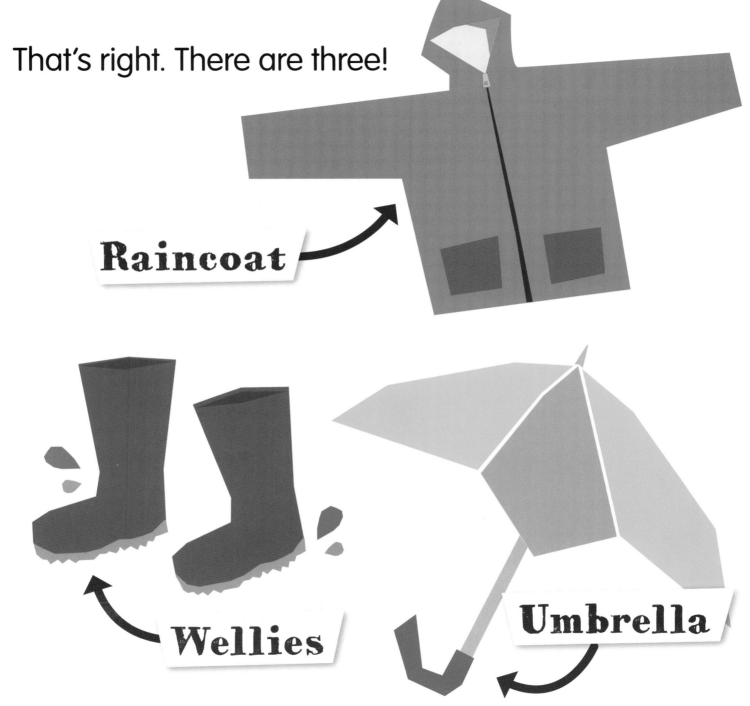

Raincoat

Wellies

Umbrella

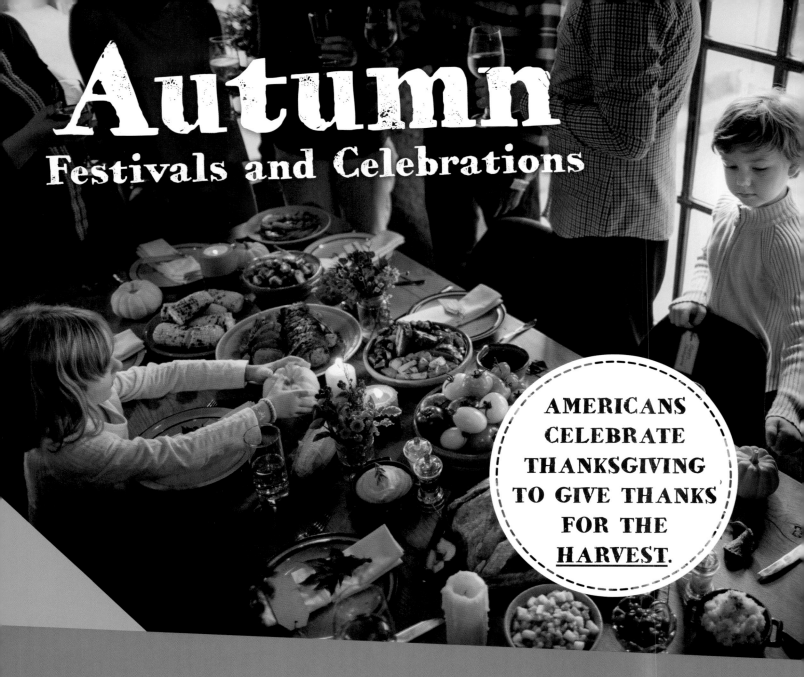

Autumn
Festivals and Celebrations

AMERICANS CELEBRATE THANKSGIVING TO GIVE THANKS FOR THE HARVEST.

Around the world there are many festivals and celebrations in autumn.

China celebrates the Moon Festival. It takes place when the Moon is at its brightest and roundest.

LANTERNS ARE LIT DURING THE MOON FESTIVAL.

HOW MANY COLOURS CAN YOU SEE?

The United Kingdom celebrates Bonfire Night by setting off fireworks and sparklers.

12

Certain festivals in autumn have <u>traditional</u> food.

IN AMERICA,
A ROAST TURKEY
IS SERVED ON
THANKSGIVING.

Autumn Food

Squash

Gourd

ORANGE PUMPKINS, GREEN GOURDS, AND YELLOW SQUASHES ALL GROW WELL IN AUTUMN.

Many different types of squash are <u>in season</u> during autumn.

14

In the Chinese Moon Festival, people eat moon cakes.

Sweet Pastry

Thick Sweet Bean Paste

Autumn
Play

In autumn, there are lots of different leaves
to play with.

When it rains there are lots of puddles to jump in.

Plants in Autumn

THESE SEEDS FALL LIKE TINY HELICOPTERS!

Sycamore trees shed their seeds in autumn.

The Chinese lantern plant turns bright orange in autumn.

THE BERRIES GROW INSIDE!

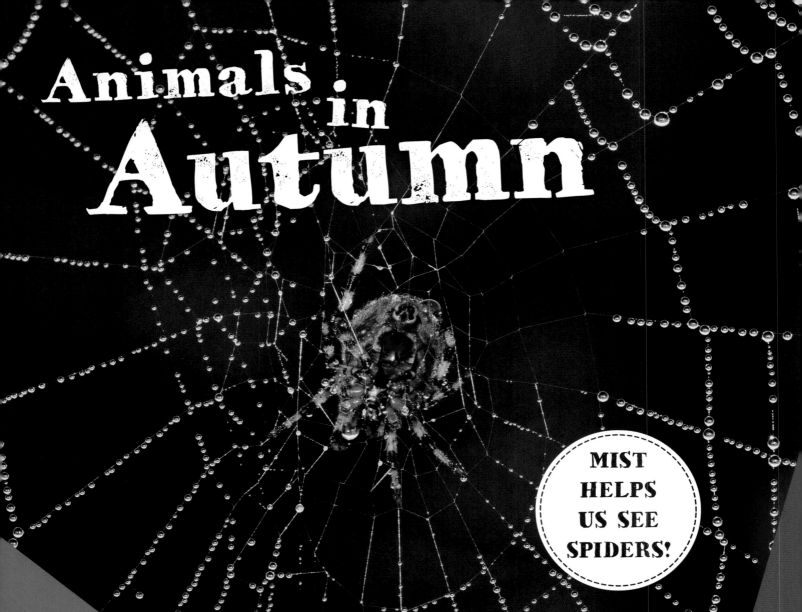

Animals in Autumn

MIST HELPS US SEE SPIDERS!

On autumn mornings the weather gets misty.
Mist is a cloud of tiny water droplets.

In autumn, squirrels collect nuts and seeds.
They dig holes to hide them in.

THIS WAY,
THE SQUIRREL
WILL HAVE
FOOD ALL
WINTER!

21

What Comes Next?

As autumn comes to an end, the weather gets colder and daytime gets shorter.

Autumn is becoming… winter!

23

GLOSSARY

harvest — the crops gathered from farming

in season — when a plant grows best

temperature — how hot a person, place or object is

traditional — a very old behaviour or belief

waterproofs — clothes that water can't pass through

INDEX

24